POEMS
for
Sight~Word
Practice

With Month-by-Month
Activities

by Laureen Reynolds

Crystal Springs
BOOKS
A division of SDE Staff Development for Educators

Peterborough, New Hampshire

Published by Crystal Springs Books
A division of Staff Development for Educators (SDE)
10 Sharon Road, PO Box 500
Peterborough, NH 03458
1-800-321-0401
www.crystalsprings.com
www.sde.com

© 2004 Laureen Reynolds
Published 2004
Printed in the United States of America
08 07 06 05   2 3 4 5

ISBN: 1-884548-69-5

Library of Congress Cataloging-in-Publication Data

Reynolds, Laureen, 1969-
  Poems for sight-word practice : with month-by-month activities / by Laureen Reynolds.
     p. cm.
  ISBN 1-884548-69-5
  1. Reading (Elementary)—Whole-word method. 2. Reading (Elementary)—Activity programs. 3. Children's poetry. I. Title.
  LB1573.37.R49 2004
  372.46'2—dc22

                    2004027148

Art Director, Designer, and Production Coordinator: Soosen Dunholter
Illustrator: Joyce Orchard Garamella

Contents

Introduction 5
   How to Use This Book 6

August/September
   Getting Ready 8
      Activities 9
   The Crayon Box 10
      Activities 11

October
   Fall Leaves 12
      Activities 13
   Choosing 14
      Activities 15

November
   Families 16
      Activities 17
   Turkey Troubles 18
      Activities 19

December
   Cookies 20
      Activities 21
   The World Over 22
      Activities 23

January
   My Snow 24
      Activities 25
   The Mitten Box 26
      Activities 27

February
   Mr. Bo Dragon 28
      Activities 29
   Too Sweet 30
      Activities 31

March
   Lion Hunt 32
      Activities 33
   Invite the Wind 34
      Activities 35

April
   Pond Poem 36
      Activities 37
   Batches of Hatches 38
      Activities 39

May
   The Honeybee 40
      Activities 41
   Watermelon Wait 42
      Activities 43

June
   Fish Wish 44
      Activities 45
   Fireflies 46
      Activities 47

Reproducibles 48

Dedication

To my parents, for starting me on this writing journey so many years ago, and to my husband, for paving the road with love and filling the potholes with encouragement.

Introduction

Children, with their sense of wonder and limitless imaginations, and poetry, with its few but powerful words, are an unbeatable combination. Reading instruction and poetry can also be a winning combination if you have the right poems. *Poems for Sight-Word Practice* is aimed at young learners who are just beginning their literary journeys as readers and writers. The poems are written using sight-word vocabulary that will build a foundation for future reading success yet with a simplicity that will attract even the most reluctant reader. The rhymes, predictable patterns, humor, and unexpected twists in these poems will escort students into the world of reading with no more than a gentle nudge.

The reasons for using sight-word poems in the classroom are many. They provide a good model when read aloud, they offer repeated exposure to valuable high-frequency words, and they lure even struggling readers, all the while promoting the fun, silliness, and imagination that good poetry can conjure up. The succinct and lighthearted nature of these poems ensures students a positive association with poetry and provides them with the kind of successful reading experience that traditional text may not be able to supply.

This energizing and valuable tool for teaching vocabulary and reading fluency also offers activities that support word-building, sentence development, fine and gross motor skills, and cross-curricular concepts. In addition to building a priceless sight-word vocabulary, your students will develop the confidence and fluency that come from successful literary endeavors while discovering the remarkable pleasure that can emerge from a good poem. Once children begin to enjoy the reading process through these poems, they will seek more opportunities to engage with print. Be ready for the reading explosion.

During my ten years of teaching in primary-grade classrooms, I have seen many a reading bandwagon load up and traverse the hallways, only to be replaced by another in a year or two. While the educational powers that be were deciding which way to go next, I was determined to address the needs and gaps with which I struggled in prescribed reading materials and instructional practices. The poems in this book have worked with every Title I, special education, and gifted child I have had the privilege of teaching. These tried-and-true activities debuted in my own first-grade classrooms over the past five years, and I am delighted to pass them along to you. When using this book, remember: The job of any educator is to propagate a vast curiosity and desire for knowledge that will feed and grow eternal learners. Poetry is a wonderful place to start.

How to Use This Book

Poems for Sight-Word Practice consists of 20 poems, two for each school month. Since some schools begin the year in August instead of September, I have combined those two months. Each poem is accompanied by four activities: three arranged by group size (individual, small group, and whole group) and one extension. If you will need materials that you might not ordinarily have on hand, these are listed alongside the activity.

To make the poems easily accessible and reproducible, each one has been printed in black-and-white as well as duplicated in the back of the book as a full-page color transparency. In addition, every page in the book, including all the transparencies, is perforated. To guard against ripping when removing pages from the book, we suggest that you first crease the perforated edge and then pull the page slowly and carefully along the perforation with one hand while pressing down toward the binding of the book with the other hand. When re-moving a transparency page, it also helps to work from back to front. Start with the front cover of the book face down, open the book from the back cover, find the transparency you want to remove, and proceed as described above.

The following suggestions apply to any of the poems included here:

- Make enlarged copies of the poems on chart paper and/or use the transparencies provided. The larger size will allow for easy choral reading, effective left-to-right/return-sweep modeling, and hands-on, one-to-one correspondence for beginning readers. Be sure to always use nonpermanent markers when writing on the transparencies.

- Make blank books by using 9" x 12" colored construction paper and 8½" x 11" sheets of copy paper. Staple 20 sheets of copy paper between two pieces of construction paper. You may need a heavy-duty stapler for this, but if one is not available, simply reduce the number of pages and make several blank books for each child for the year. Each week, distribute photocopies of a poem for the children to cut out and glue into their books. You may want to include some appropriately lined paper for your young poets as they experiment with writing verse on their own.

- When reading a poem from a pocket chart or chart paper, make pictures to replace particularly difficult words, such as *watermelon*, *penguin*, *pumpkin*, and *candle*. This will increase your emerging readers' confidence and success.

- Place individual letter cards in a hat or bag and have each student choose one. Ask students to scan a poem of your choosing—or theirs—for words that begin with those letters and to write them down. Have them read their lists to you or their partners.

- Pick a poem, select words that you want to focus on, and write the words on index cards. Make a duplicate set of these words. Set up memory or concentration games around the classroom, making sure that all cards at each game location are matched pairs. Tell the children to take turns playing the game. The first child turns over two cards; if they match, she keeps the pair and gets another turn. Each time she turns over two cards, she must read the words revealed, whether they match or not. Explain to students that they want to try to remember which cards have been turned over and where they are within the grid so that they can find matching cards when it is their turn.

- Give each student a blank laminated bingo grid with 9 to 16 squares. Supply children with dry-erase markers and tell them to fill in each square on their grids with a word from a particular poem. Play a bingo-style game in which you read a word and they cover it if it is on their cards. Once a child calls out "Bingo!," he must read aloud each word in the winning line on his grid.

As you use this book, I'm sure you will discover your own favorite activities and create new ones as well. Enjoy!

Getting Ready

The bus is near,
I need my sock.
The bus is near,
It's up the block!
The bus is near,
Can't find my shoe.
The bus is near,
What will I do?
The bus is HERE,
I've got to run!
It's time for school,
Let's have some fun!

ACTIVITIES FOR "GETTING READY"

Individual:

Make a letter book for the letter *Bb* in the shape of a bus (see reproducible). Use construction paper for the front and back covers and staple blank pages inside for the kids to fill with pictures cut out of old magazines, with drawings, or with words they can write that begin with *Bb*. Accept invented spelling for this activity as long as *Bb* is in the initial slot.

Materials:

bus reproducible (see page 48)

construction paper

Small Group:

Distribute one index card to each child in the group. Have children write one of the words *The, bus,* or *is* on their cards. Give them paper copies of the poem and ask them to find and circle their words as many times as they can. You can have them write their words down on a small wipe-off board or say them aloud each time they come across them. You can also reinforce word sequence and the concepts of complete and incomplete sentences during this activity. Have children stand, each with an index card in hand, so that they make the phrase *The bus is*. Then ask them to brainstorm a word or phrase to complete the sentence, write it on an index card, and read it again.

Materials:

index cards

Whole Group:

Using the transparency and a pointer, model an appropriate reading pace for the children to follow. After some practice with the poem, speed up or slow down the pointing sporadically and challenge the children to keep up. Your students will get a laugh out of this and some good reading practice, too!

Materials:

teacher's photo biography

My Teacher Sleeps in School by Leatie and Ellen Weiss

Literature Extension:

Over the summer, prepare a short picture tour of your life that you can share with your students during the first few days of school. Include pictures of your home, pets, hobbies, family members, and anything else appropriate. When school begins, read *My Teacher Sleeps in School* to your class. Afterwards, share your photo biography. The story is wonderful and silly, and your students will thoroughly enjoy finding out about their new teacher's "real life."

The Crayon Box

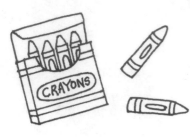

Let's use blue
To spread the sky.
Brown helps draw
A nest up high.
Green makes grass
In May or June.
White can show
The fullest moon.
Purple's for
A juicy grape.
Red shows off
A hero's cape.
Black brings in
The dark of night.
Orange holds
A pumpkin's light.

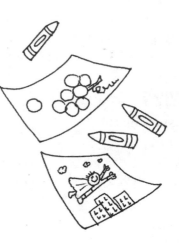

ACTIVITIES FOR "THE CRAYON BOX"

Individual:

Distribute copies of the poem and have children trace over each color word with its corresponding crayon. Your students will enjoy using a supersized version of the poem while learning those all-important color words.

Materials:

enlarged photocopy of the poem for each child

Small Group:

Read the poem together. Give several color puddles (about 1" x 2") to each student in the group. On an enlarged version of the poem, have each child tape her puddle over the corresponding color word. Read it again with the puddles in place. Groups of four work well for this activity, so that each child has a chance to place two color puddles.

The Crayon Box

Let's use 🟦 to spread the sky.
🟤 helps draw a nest up high
🟩 makes grass in May or June.
⬜ can show the fullest moon.
🟣 for a juicy grape

Materials:

colored construction paper puddles

Whole Group:

Using the transparency and a nonpermanent marker, ask each child to come to the projector and circle a word that he can read/teach to the class. Students who have not yet developed a sight-word vocabulary can pick a letter and teach its sound. Then have children determine which color in their crayon boxes is not mentioned in the poem (yellow) and together brainstorm a line for yellow to add to the poem.

Science/Social Studies Extension:

Enlist your students' help to unwrap pieces of old or broken crayons. Place a few crayon pieces of different colors into each section of an old mini muffin tin and place in a toaster oven at about 200°. Bake until the wax crayons have melted completely. Carefully remove the tin from the toaster and set it aside to cool; then pop out the crayons and place them in your art area. Your students will enjoy the new multicolored crayons, and you will have provided them with an excellent lesson in recycling!

Materials:

mini muffin tin
toaster oven

Fall Leaves

One is orange,
Two are brown,
Three look yellow
On the ground.

Three are green,
Two bright red,
One just fell
Upon my head!

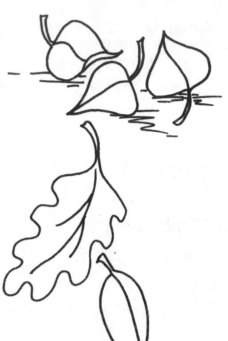

ACTIVITIES FOR "FALL LEAVES"

Individual:

Based on the age of the children with whom you are working, have them make number-word books using leaves as the theme. Very young children could use numbers 1–3 and draw leaves using a real leaf as the model. Older children could use numbers 1–10 and trace smaller leaves, or even 1–20 and do leaf rubbings. This is a great way to bring science, math, and language arts together.

Materials:

variety of real fall leaves (or artificial leaves)

Small Group:

Have each child in the group trace her arm and hand (with fingers spread out) onto a sheet of brown construction paper to make the trunk and branches of a

tree. Tell students to cut out their "trees" and glue them onto a sheet of light blue construction paper. Provide a supply of small colored paper leaves and have the children write a member of the "all" word family on each leaf. They should fill in a word on as many leaves as they can and glue them onto their trees. The trees make a terrific bulletin board display for the autumn season and a valuable "all" family word wall.

Materials:

colored construction paper (brown and light blue)

small colored paper leaves

Whole Group:

Read the poem together from the transparency; then have the children make a list of the numbers and colors of the leaves mentioned in the poem. Take your students on a nature walk to collect leaves according to their lists. If your climate does not allow for authentic leaf gathering, use paper, preserved, or artificial leaves. This activity is a simple introduction to list writing—something everyone can use! Emphasize to your students that a list is usually written in vertical form.

Each list should read:
1 — orange
2 — brown
3 — yellow
3 — green
2 — red

Art/Writing Extension:

Have each child glue a leaf of his choice onto a sheet of construction paper. Using the leaf as the trunk of a body, have children add arms, legs, wings, a head, or anything else they wish, to their leaf characters. Ask them to write or tell a story about their leafy creations.

Materials:

variety of leaves, real or artificial

light blue construction paper

Choosing

Is this the one?
I just don't know.
It must be right,
And look just so.

Should it be short?
Should it be tall?
I must choose now,
It's time, it's fall!

I look at each,
Both up and down,
To find the best
In all the town.

I've got it now.
It's quite a catch!
I found it at
The pumpkin patch!

ACTIVITIES FOR "CHOOSING"

Individual:

Draw each stage of the pumpkin's growth cycle on a separate square of paper and give each student a complete set. Ask children to color the stages appropriately and then glue them in sequence to standard sentence strips. If there is time, they can tell friends about each picture.

Hint: Save this piece and compare it with a similar watermelon activity you and your students can do in May. Your class will be pleased with their progress.

Materials:

pumpkin's growth cycle
  (see
  www.enchantedlearning.com
  or
  www.scienceforfamilies.all
  info-about.com)

3" x 3" squares of paper

Small Group:

Precut a hole in the top of the pumpkin and then replace the cover. Cut out the shape of a pumpkin from the orange paper and ask the group members to describe what they see and feel on the outside of the real pumpkin. Record their answers on the front side of the paper pumpkin. After a few minutes, remove the cover of the pumpkin and ask children to describe what they see, feel, or even smell on the inside of the pumpkin. Record these answers on the back side of the paper pumpkin. If there is time, have each group member estimate the number of seeds inside the pumpkin.

Materials:

real pumpkin

orange colored paper

Whole Group:

Read the poem together from the transparency. Afterward, have each child come up and mark a word in the poem that contains the letter *Ii*. Read all the words marked as a group. Listen for and discuss the different sounds of *Ii* in words. Tell students to remember this when they are trying to sound out an unknown word. Use this opportunity to remind your students that the pronoun *I* is always uppercase.

Culinary Extension:

Roast or panfry the pumpkin seeds and enjoy them with your students. This is a great way to incorporate a discussion of the five senses into a language lesson. (Check with your facilities manager before using a toaster oven in your classroom and with your school nurse for any allergy concerns pertinent to your student population.)

Materials:

toaster oven or electric
  skillet

Families

Some have one,
Two, three, or four.
Some have many,
Many more.

Some live far,
And others near,
But all of them
Are very dear.

ACTIVITIES FOR "FAMILIES"

Individual:
On a piece of white paper, have each child draw a shape that roughly resembles the outline of her house, apartment building, mobile home, etc. Then have each student draw a picture of her family inside that shape. Ask your students to write or tell one thing about each family member they drew.

Small Group:
In advance, have each child bring a family photo to school. Request that the picture be labeled with the names and ages of each person shown, if possible. Using the ages on each child's photo, give them math puzzles to do, such as ordering the ages, adding or subtracting two ages, and picking out odd or even ages. For a challenge, see whether anyone can add more than two ages together. This is a wonderful link between home and school.

Materials:

photograph of child's
  family

Whole Group:
Use the transparency to do a choral reading of the poem. Highlight the number words or words that tell "how many." Afterward, graph the number of children in your class with families of two, three, four, or more members.

Literature Extension:
Read the book to your class and discuss what kinds of things you might need if you were going away. Afterward, distribute construction paper and a pipe cleaner to each child. Ask students to staple a pipe cleaner to the top of the paper in a half-circle to make a handle. Have your students draw the things they would take with them on a trip to a relative's house.

Hint: Use paper grocery bags instead of construction paper and have children draw on the blank sides.

Materials:

*The Bag I'm Taking to
  Grandma's* by Shirley
  Neitzel

light tan construction
  paper

pipe cleaners

Turkey Troubles

I ran into a turkey
Last night down by the lake.
I asked if he would join me
For a bit of chocolate cake.

He seemed a little shaky.
He jumped at every sound.
And when I closed the
door too hard
He fell onto the ground.

"Tomorrow is Thanksgiving!"
With fear that turkey said.
But Mom said not to worry,
And we had ham instead.

Activities for "Turkey Troubles"

Individual:

Have each child make a list of the foods she and her family have on Thanksgiving. Ask students to compare theirs with a friend's list and note any differences. If appropriate, ask children to put their listed items in alphabetical order. You can also graph the results to find the most popular (and unpopular!) holiday foods.

Small Group:

Ask group members to talk about one of their family traditions and their favorite part of the Thanksgiving meal. If you start by sharing your own, you will provide a good model and the children will enjoy knowing a little more about you.

Whole Group:

Display the transparency and read the poem with your class. Then ask volunteers to come up and mark all of the two-syllable words. After students have identified them, read the words as a group and clap out the syllables.

Community Extension:

Conduct a food drive to benefit a local nonprofit organization. (Your school nurse should be able to direct you to a worthwhile cause.) Ask each family to donate a few cans and/or boxes of nonperishable food. Encourage the children, with their parents' permission and supervision, to ask their neighbors to donate as well. Once they have gathered all the food, have students decorate Thanksgiving placemats made of construction paper (which you can laminate) or vinyl (which you can purchase inexpensively at your local fabric store). Community food pantries or assistance programs can use the placemats to brighten up the holiday for someone less fortunate. Be sure to check with your school's administration before doing this activity.

Materials:

colored construction paper or pieces of vinyl

Cookies

I have one.
I eat it fast.

I take two.
They will not last.

I grab three.
Mom does not see.

Now it's four.
May I have more?

Mom says no.
I don't know why.

I think I'll give
My dad a try.

ACTIVITIES FOR "COOKIES"

Individual:

Cut out ten 6" circles from the paper and staple them together to make a blank book, titled *The "ook" Book*, for each child. The book should be round like a cookie. Ask your students to color the covers to resemble their favorite cookies and to write a word from the *ook* family on each page. Encourage your more advanced students to use blends and digraphs at the beginning of their words.

Materials:

white construction or copy paper

Small Group:

Using the transparency with a few children at a time, ask each one to come to the projector, underline a long- or a short-vowel word (whichever you choose), and then say a word that rhymes with it.

Whole Group:

Be sure to check for any food allergies before doing this activity. Sample two kinds of cookies with your class; then use a Venn diagram to compare the two. Your students will appreciate the treat, and you will have a wonderful technique for introducing and reviewing adjectives.

Materials:

Two different kinds of cookies

Culinary Extension:

With your students as helpers, measure and mix the ingredients, and bake the cookies as directed. Enjoy these freshly baked goodies at snack time. (Check with your facilities manager before using a toaster oven in your classroom and with your school nurse for any allergy concerns pertinent to your student population.)

Materials:

simple cookie recipe and ingredients

measuring spoons and cups

mixing bowls and other necessary utensils

baking sheets

toaster oven (or ask permission to use school cafeteria oven)

The World Over

December's the time
For all to learn
Why handbells ring
And candles burn.

December's the time
For all to know
Why people sing
And small lights glow.

December's the time
For all to hold
Sweet hopes and dreams
For young and old.

ACTIVITIES FOR "THE WORLD OVER"

Individual:

No matter what cultures your students celebrate, ask each one to illustrate a favorite part of that celebration and to share it with a classmate or with the whole group at a later date. This activity is sure to broaden your students' understanding of global holidays.

Hint: If everyone in your classroom celebrates the same holiday, take a trip to the library or go online to find out how children around the globe celebrate their major holidays, which do not necessarily have to fall in December.

Small Group:

Write the names of the months on index cards, one month per card. Give each child in the group three or four cards. Read them together; then have all of the children in the group sort them by number of syllables. Ask them to make observations about the results, such as *January* and *February* both having four syllables.

Materials:

index cards

Whole Group:

Using the transparency, read the poem to or with the whole group. Underline the word *all* each time it is spoken. Then ask for volunteers to write words that rhyme with *all* around the border of the poem, in any direction they choose.

Social Studies Extension:

Read the book to your class; then choose five to seven countries from various regions of the world (Europe, Africa, Asia, and so on) and discuss the ways children celebrate in those places. As you begin studying each country, pin a flag or some other marker to that spot on a bulletin board map. Be sure you mark the spot that represents your hometown as well. This is a great lesson in geography and cultural diversity.

Materials:

Children Just Like Me: Celebrations! by Anabel and Barnabus Kindersley

world map

tiny flags

pushpins or tacks

My Snow

Down it came,
In the night.
Just for me,
New and white.

Still it comes,
As I play.
My best friend
For today.

Make three balls,
Build them high.
Then I stop
To thank the sky.

Activities for "My Snow"

Individual:

Set up an art center where children can make old-fashioned paper snowflakes by folding and cutting white paper. Model how to do this first, depending on the age of your students. Use these frosty masterpieces to decorate windows, doors, or ceilings, and create your own winter wonderland.

Small Group:

Make flip books with three or four children at a time. Divide a sheet of any size paper in half with a black vertical line. On the right side of the line, have your students write *ow*. On the left side of the line, staple squares of blank paper. Ask children to write a letter, blend, or digraph on each square to make a new *ow* word. If time allows, ask each child to pick one or two words to illustrate on the back side of the flip book. More advanced students may point out that *ow* has two sounds. A brief discussion about this is appropriate. Students who are able may choose to do two books, each illustrating one *ow* sound.

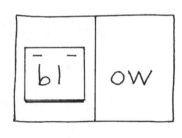

Whole Group:

Display the transparency and read the poem with your students several times. Brainstorm actions to go with each line or set of lines. For example, children can act out the line "Down it came" by wiggling their fingers in the air, starting above their heads and traveling down to the ground. Children can show "In the night" simply by resting their heads on their hands with palms together. Read it again solo while the children act as mimes, using the actions they have created.

Science/Math Extension:

Gather a bucket of snow from outdoors or fill a bucket with ice cubes if real snow is not available. Have children estimate how long it will take for the snow or ice cubes to melt. Ask students to record their guesses in hours and minutes on small squares of paper and place them in a jar. After everything has melted, reveal the closest guess.

Materials:

bucket of snow or ice cubes

The Mitten Box

I pick a pair
When I go there.
They may not match,
But I don't care.
The left one's green
With yellow spots.
The right one has
Pink polka dots.
And even though
They aren't the same,
They work just fine
For winter's game.

ACTIVITIES FOR "THE MITTEN BOX"

Individual:

Supply an art center with mitten tracers, oak tag, felt, yarn, and pom-poms. Have each child design and decorate an original pair of mittens.

Small Group:

Brainstorm rhymes for the word *box* with group members. Words with *ox* or *ocks* at the end are acceptable. Ask children to write each word that fits the rhyme on an index card. You may help them with correct spelling. Once the group has recorded a number of words, bring out a shoe box labeled *ox* and a large paper sock labeled *ocks*. Have students read and sort each rhyming word into the appropriate container.

Whole Group:

Ask each of the children to bring one of her mittens to school in a paper lunch bag (to ensure secrecy), with a written clue about herself stuck inside the mitten. Collect the bags as they arrive and place the mittens in a box. Using the transparency as your guide, read the poem as a group. Afterward, bring out the mitten box and have each child take one mitten other than her own. Have each student in turn read the clue inside her mitten and try to guess to whom it belongs.

Math Extension:

Write a sequence of numbers you are practicing with your class on 4" x 6" mittens cut from construction paper. Give one mitten to each child. Tie a length of string or rope to two things in the classroom to serve as a temporary clothesline, and make sure it is low enough for your students to reach. Arm each child with a clothespin and ask him to pin his number up in sequence with the numbers you have already placed on the line. Continue until students have pinned up all the numbers, and then recite the sequence aloud as a group.

Materials:

mitten shapes for tracing

oak tag

felt, yarn, pom-poms

Materials:

index cards

shoe box

large paper sock

Materials:

colored construction paper

string or rope

clothespins

Mr. Bo Dragon

I have a friend,
His name is Bo.
He is not like
The others, though.

He likes to jump,
To skip and run.
We sing and dance
Till day is done.

Just Bo and I,
That's how it is.
For he is mine,
And I am his.

ACTIVITIES FOR "MR. BO DRAGON"

Individual:

Have each student draw a picture of an imaginary friend she would like to have. Then ask the children, in turn, to write or tell the class about their friends.

Small Group:

Supply each child with a copy of the reproducible. Have each student write *dr* in the body of the dragon and a letter or letters on each plate to complete a word. Some suggestions for words to make with young readers and writers are: *drip, drop, draw, drink, dry, drill,* and *drag*. Encourage more advanced students to create longer words.

Materials:

Mr. Bo Dragon reproducible (see page 48)

Whole Group:

Display the transparency and ask the children to look and listen for the action words in the poem (*jump, skip, run, sing, dance*). Ask volunteers to come up and color those words green. Then substitute other action words, suggested by your students, for the ones in the poem, but be sure to keep *run* in its spot to preserve the rhyme. If you want to build movement into the lesson, let students act out the new verbs.

Writing Extension:

Have each child write a plan for a "perfect day" with his best friend. Encourage students to include details about places they would go, things they would see and do, and at what times of the day these events would occur.

Too Sweet

My mom gave me a valentine.
My teacher did the same.
My friends each gave me one as well.
The cards all had my name.

I ate the chocolate heart from Mom,
The goodies from Miss West.
I even ate a lollipop
That said, "You are the Best!"

I tried to eat a little more
Of all that yummy stuff,
But Mom said, "No more for today,
I think you're sweet enough."

ACTIVITIES FOR "TOO SWEET"

Individual:

Supply each child with any number of hearts. Tell the children to write a "sweet sentence," putting one word on each heart. Then have them glue their hearts together in the correct order of the sentence. Model this for your students by making a sentence about the class, putting each of the following words in a heart: *My, class, is,* and *kind.* Brainstorm a list of words that students may want to use in their sweet sentences and list them on the board or on chart paper. Have them help you with the spelling where appropriate. The kids can use these as valentines for family or friends.

Materials:
pastel-colored construction paper hearts

Small Group:

Invite several children to sit with you at a table. On a large wipe-off board, write the word *valentine.* Give each child a sheet of paper, with each letter in the word *valentine* written inside a heart. Have the students cut out the hearts. Then ask each group member to make small words out of the letters in the big word *valentine.* Ask the children to spell the words and record answers on the wipe-off board.

Whole Group:

Display the transparency and read the poem together. Have each child come up and draw a heart around a long-vowel word and read it aloud to the class.

Community Extension:

Arrange for a local dentist to come and speak to the children about the importance of eating healthy foods and brushing, flossing, and seeing their dentists regularly. See whether your school nurse can acquire a giant toothbrush, and ask your physical education teacher for a jump rope to act as a giant piece of dental floss. Have the dentist demonstrate proper flossing techniques by asking children to stand in a row and then "flossing" between them as you would real teeth.

Lion Hunt

I've been looking
For a lion.
They say he's very near.

I sneak around
Each corner 'cause
I don't want him to hear.

I look each day
And every night.
Please help, I'm in a jam.

I've been looking
For a lion,
But can only find a lamb!

ACTIVITIES FOR "LION HUNT"

Individual:

Ask each child to write two or three completions to: *If I had a lion, I would_____*. Have students share their responses with the class at a designated time. You will be surprised at how creative they can be! Let each child pick one idea and illustrate it. Combine all the illustrations into a class book for your library. Your students will no doubt visit it again and again.

Small Group:

Make your own drawing of a lion's body, cut out the individual parts, and give each child in the group one or more of the parts. Have each group member tape or glue his lion parts onto a mural-size piece of paper. After the group has assembled its lion's body, tell the children to brainstorm adjectives that describe the lion and write the words around his body. Display the mural in the hallway and encourage passersby to add their own adjectives to it, using a marker tied to a string.

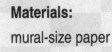

Materials:

mural-size paper

Whole Group:

Using the transparency, ask volunteers to locate and circle vowel couplets such as *ea, ou, ee*, and so on. Have each volunteer read the word she has found, and ask the rest of the class to identify the sounds the vowels make.

Social Development/Literature Extension:

Read the book to your students. Afterward, discuss the character's problem and the story's outcome. Then have everyone, including you, write a personal hope for the future on the paper flowers. Each one should start: *I hope I bloom into a better _____*. Use the flowers to make a bulletin board or hallway display. At the end of the year, see which students have bloomed into whatever they had hoped for.

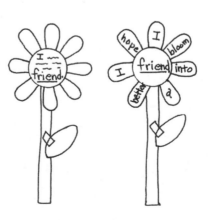

Materials:

Leo the Late Bloomer by Robert Kraus

paper flowers cut from construction paper

Invite the Wind

When you go
Outside today,
Ask the wind
If he will play.

When you start
Out for a walk,
Ask the wind
If he will talk.

When you want
To play a game,
Ask the wind
To call your name.

But once at home,
Doors open wide,
Don't ask the wind
To come inside.

ACTIVITIES FOR "INVITE THE WIND"

Individual:

Supply each child with a graph and one each of some small objects like paper clips, crayons, blocks, tissues, cotton balls, and so forth. Have him write down the name of each object (or draw a picture) at the bottom of the graph and then record the number of puffs it takes to blow the object across a desk.

Materials:

blank graph for each child

Small Group:

Read one of the stories aloud with small groups of children in a quiet spot in your room. Then ask group members to retell it by taking turns adding details in sequence until the story ends. This is a great way to build reading comprehension in young children.

Materials:

The Wind Blew by Pat Hutchins, *Henry and Mudge and the Wild Wind* by Cynthia Rylant, or another story about the wind

Whole Group:

Display the transparency and ask a group of children to read a line or section of the poem. Afterward, have volunteers write question words around the poem.

Literature Extension:

Introduce the students to Christina Rossetti (1830–94) and her poem. This provides great opportunities for choral reading, illustrating, acting out lines from the poem, etc.

Materials:

"Who Has Seen the Wind?" by Christina Rossetti

Pond Poem

At the pond
You can jump
With green bullfrogs
On old wet stumps.

At the pond
You can ride
A beaver's back
From side to side.

At the pond
You can hear
A cricket's song
Both far and near.

At the pond
You can think,
Does a duck
Need to blink?

ACTIVITIES FOR "POND POEM"

Materials:

chart paper

Individual:

Reproduce the poem on a piece of chart paper. During individual free time, have each child draw a pond animal and glue it to the chart paper to decorate the border. When all the children have added their pictures, they will have created a thematic decorative border.

Small Group:

Give each group member several sentence strips, each containing a different line from the poem. Have children work together within their group to place the poem back in order in a pocket chart. Read it together to ensure accuracy.

Whole Group:

Display the transparency and read the poem aloud several times as a group. Then line up the children shoulder to shoulder, facing the poem. Have each child read a line of the poem in turn until the end. If necessary, repeat the poem until each child has read a line.

Science/Technology Extension:

Visit *www.enchantedlearning.com* with your students and type *frog life cycle* into the "Search" box to bring up a simple diagram. Don't stick to just frogs, though—you will find printable books and diagrams of many pond inhabitants there. Always be sure to supervise your students' travels on the Internet, and check with your technology coordinator for other appropriate sites.

Batches of Hatches

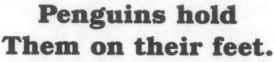

Penguins hold
Them on their feet.

Chicken eggs
Need lots of heat.

Shark eggs look
Just like a purse.

Frog eggs look
A little worse.

Duck eggs crack
And even roll.

Turtles lay
Them in a hole.

Pretty songbirds
Lay eggs, too.

A robin's egg
Is oh so blue.

Activities for "Batches of Hatches"

Individual:

Give each child a copy of the poem and ask her to highlight the words with silent vowels.

Materials:

photocopies of the poem

Small Group:

Cut egg shapes out of the paper. Choose words from the poem and write each one on a paper egg, leaving slight spaces between the letters. Then cut the eggs apart so that they look as though they have cracked open. Give some parts to each of the children and have them put the words back together. For younger children, you may want to cut the eggs in two pieces only, but challenge older students with longer words and multiple pieces.

Materials:

white construction paper

Whole Group:

Display the transparency and read the poem aloud as a group. Ask volunteers to come up individually and circle the name of an egg-laying animal. After students have identified all of them, enlist their help to place the animal names in alphabetical order.

Science/Social Studies Extension:

Provide pictures of each animal's habitat and have children help you place each oviparous (egg-laying) creature into its proper environment. Have a map or globe available to point out the location of each habitat as you place the animal.

Materials:

pictures of animals' habitats

map or globe

The Honeybee

I can see
A honeybee
Go in and out
Of that old tree.

I can see
A honeybee
Fly up and down
My garden's sea.

I can see
A honeybee
Jump rose to rose
So fast and free.

Then I see
That honeybee
Rest for a while
Right next to me.

ACTIVITIES FOR "THE HONEYBEE"

Individual:

Give an enlarged copy of the reproducible to each child. Have students write words that rhyme with *bee* inside each stripe and on each wing. Challenge them to think of words that are not used in the poem, and encourage them to use initial blends like *fr*, *spr*, *fl*, and so forth.

Small Group:

With a few children at a time, brainstorm words that begin with *Bb*. Write tongue twisters using those words. An example is: *Bumble bees bounce between beautiful blue blossoms.* This activity will stretch your students' vocabulary and give everyone a chance to giggle.

Whole Group:

Display the transparency and read the poem as a group. Have volunteers come up and circle all of the long *e* words with a yellow nonpermanent marker. Help them notice the spelling difference between *see* and *sea*. Then make a column on each side of the poem, marking one *ee* and one *ea*. Use words from the poem and words your students generate to fill each column. Words that have either vowel couplet at the beginning, in the middle, or at the end are acceptable answers. The sounds these letters create together are the focus.

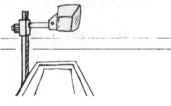

Technology Extension:

Visit *www.honey.com/kids* with your students for fun bee facts and photographs, a list of bee experts you can e-mail with questions, honey recipes, games, a virtual tour of a beekeeper's activities, and more.

Watermelon Wait

Just yesterday I planted
A watermelon seed.
So I'll be sure to give it
Whatever it might need.

I'll water it each morning
And give it lots of sun.
I'll pull up any weeds that grow,
Then watch till day is done.

Now, if I do it all just right,
Soon I will see a sign.
I'll know my little seedling
Is growing up just fine.

ACTIVITIES FOR "WATERMELON WAIT"

Individual:

Cut out a large green oval and a slightly smaller pink oval, glue the two together, and attach to a bulletin board. Cut out a few large black seeds and glue them to the watermelon. Cut out as many white seeds as there are children in your classroom, making sure that the seeds are

large enough for children to write on. Give the children each a white seed and ask them to write a word that rhymes with *seed*. Then have them, one by one, glue their seed/rhyming word onto the watermelon.

Materials:

red or pink, green, black, and white construction paper

Small Group:

Give each member of the group a picture that depicts one part of a plant's life cycle. Have children work together to put the pictures in order and to create a label or a sentence to go with each one.

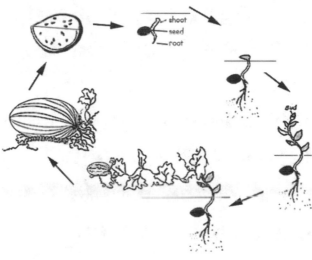

Materials:

pictures of plant's life cycle (see illustration)

Whole Group:

Using the transparency, ask the children to pick out the two-, three-, and four-syllable words from the poem and write them on a piece of chart paper or a chalkboard. Ask them to help you read and sort the words according to the number of syllables they contain.

Materials:

several whole watermelons of various sizes

bathroom scale

Math Extension:

Line the melons up on a table and leave slips of paper and a shallow dish or jar by each one. Throughout the day, remind children to guess how much each melon weighs, write it on a slip of paper, and place the paper in the appropriate container. At math time the next day, read their guesses and the melons' actual weights with your class. Afterward, slice up the watermelons for a healthy, refreshing snack.

Fish Wish

If I could make
One little wish,
I'd only want
To be a fish.

I'd want to swim,
As fishes do,
Near sunken ships
And turtles, too.

I'd wish to play
Beside the whales,
Then catch a ride
On dolphin tails.

I'd bravely dash
Past caves so dark
While watching for
A hungry shark.

ACTIVITIES FOR "FISH WISH"

Individual:

Set up a magnet center on the side of a metal desk or filing cabinet that is accessible to your students. Provide an *sh* magnet along with magnetic vowels and other popular letters. Allow each child time during the week to make words by manipulating the letters and the *sh* magnet. Remind students that *sh* can be used at the beginning, in the middle, or at the end of a word.

Materials:
magnetic letters

Small Group:

Make a fishing pole with the dowel and string, and tie the magnet to the end of the string as the "hook." Write words containing *sh* on the paper fish, and attach a paper clip to each one. Spread the fish out on the floor in a "pond" and give each group member a chance to fish for a word. If the child can read the fish she caught, she may keep it. If she cannot read it, have the group read the word together with you, and throw the fish back into the pond.

Materials:
2'-long wooden dowel
string
magnet
paper clips
small fish cut from construction paper

Whole Group:

Display the transparency and read the poem aloud, emphasizing the *sh* sound. Then ask volunteers to take turns coming forward, read any word containing the *sh* sound, and color it with a blue nonpermanent marker.

Literature Extension:

Read the book to your class. Discuss the teamwork used by the fish in the story to overcome a problem. Brainstorm real-life examples that might require teamwork, such as cleaning up the classroom, building a snowman, playing a game, and taking care of a family or classroom pet. After a brief discussion, give each child a sheet of red construction paper and take the black one for yourself. Standing together, try to make a fish similar to the one in the story.

Materials:
Swimmy by Leo Lionni
sheets of red construction paper, one for each child
sheet of black construction paper for teacher

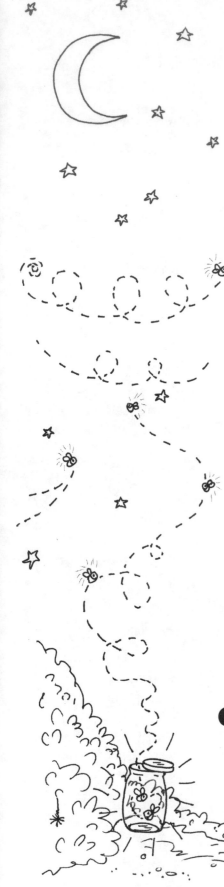

Fireflies

They always wait
Until it's night
To make their magic
Yellow light.

They seem to know
When I come near
I've got a trick
To keep them here.

I fill my jar
So they will stay
Just for a while,
Then fly away.

With one last blink
They fill the night
Like little stars.
Good night, sleep tight.

ACTIVITIES FOR "FIREFLIES"

Individual:

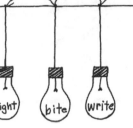

Cut out a number of lightbulbs and give a few to each child, along with a length of yarn. Ask her to write one word that rhymes with *light* on each lightbulb. Point out that before she writes, she should turn the lightbulb so that the bulb part is pointing downward. After she finishes writing, tell her to tape her lightbulbs to a piece of yarn to make a string of lights.

Materials:

lightbulbs cut from paper

lengths of yarn

Small Group:

Copy the poem onto chart paper, leaving out a number of words and allowing spaces about the size of an index card. Give each child in the group two or three index cards, with a missing word from the poem written on each one. Have members take turns placing their words in the appropriate spaces and attaching them with tape.

Materials:

index cards

Whole Group:

Display the transparency. After reading the poem together, ask volunteers to take turns coming forward and to highlight the long *i* words with a yellow nonpermanent marker.

Literature Extension:

Read the book to your class, being sure to turn the lights down low as you approach the last page. The end of this book conjures up wonderful feelings and a delightful visual surprise.

Materials:

The Very Lonely Firefly
by Eric Carle